BORDER REFLECTIONS

by the same author

THE WAY THE WIND BLOWS

BORDER
REFLECTIONS

*chiefly on the arts
of shooting and fishing*

Lord Home

Illustrations by Rodger McPhail

COLLINS
St James's Place, London
1979

William Collins Sons & Co Ltd
London · Glasgow · Sydney · Auckland
Toronto ·· Johannesburg

First published 1979
© Lord Home 1979

ISBN 0 00 216301 2

Set in Bembo
Made and Printed in Great Britain by
William Collins Sons & Co Ltd Glasgow

To my Grandsons
Rory and Matthew

CONTENTS

FOREWORD

This short book is written in the hope that it will whet the appetite of young men of today to occupy some of their leisure time with rod and gun.

It does not deal in record bags, but rather with the hunt after game-birds which can be undertaken by the individual alone with his dog, or by a party of friends who can acquire or rent a shoot where the emphasis is on variety.

I have drawn my recollections from the Lowlands of Scotland, but there are other places where with careful management and a lot of luck every column in the local game book may be filled.

Much of the lore of nature he will have to discover for himself after much walking and stalking and study of the local habits of the different species, but he may find in these pages some hints which will enable him to get on terms with his quarry more successfully than he might otherwise have done.

As for the fisherman – he is born not made, and the most that I can do is to stimulate him to put his line into the water, and keep it there even in the most unpromising conditions. He will need luck, but he will catch fish.

Whether the young man shoots or fishes or both he will move among the birds and the beasts and the mountains and valleys, and he will learn about nature's ways. He will know the excitement of anticipation, and the luxury of reminiscence, and I hope that he will conclude, as I have done, that when shooting or fishing no day can ever be dull.

CHAPTER I

Apprentice to Nature

It is scarcely surprising that the love of the chase is in the blood of the Douglases and the Homes. Away back in the fourteenth century tales were handed down from father to son of the fleetness of foot of the Black Douglas, who would run the deer to a standstill. Favourite of Robert the Bruce, he had the freedom of most of the South of Scotland, and Ettrick Forest was his particular playground whenever he was not on the more serious business of chasing the English back over the Border.

The larder of the Douglas clansmen and camp-followers was always full.

The area around Douglas had a good reputation for game, and the red deer and the wild boar even tempted Edward I of England – the 'Hammer of the Scots' – to enter hostile country. He had a shooting lodge near the present village of Crawford-john, and there he would entertain the ambassadors to the Court of St James.

On one occasion he commanded that his diplomatic guests should keep their dessert plates covered until he gave the word for the lids to be lifted. He forecast that they would be surprised by the excellence of the local 'fruits'. When the covers were removed the 'fruits' were found to be nuggets of gold from the stream which ran down from the Lead Hills.

The experience of Mary Queen of Scots at Douglas was not so happy, for she was the quarry who was hunted. She took refuge and was hidden in a small house next door to the Chapel of St Bride's, where the English had been massacred by the Black Douglas many years before. As a token of her gratitude for shelter she presented a clock to the church tower, and it is in working order to this day. She would turn in her grave if she knew that the house in which she hid was later converted into a small church for the Protestant population of Douglas.

Some 300 years later King Edward VII came to shoot grouse with my grandfather, and he occupied a butt only a mile from Crawfordjohn where Edward I used to enjoy himself. My father often told me about that October shoot. It was on a cold day with snow showers, and the King had not been well. It was one of those rare occasions when everything had gone according to plan, and large numbers of grouse had been collected in an area from which they were bound to return through the line of guns.

As the beaters started the King said that he was feeling cold, and would like to go home. Protocol demanded that everyone should go with him. My father reported that it was the only occasion on which his loyalty and that of his friends was severely strained. Lord Brackley stayed behind out of curiosity to see how the grouse would behave; when he returned he said that they had streamed through the butts in coveys and packs, without being driven. Even so the bag was 200 brace.

My recollection of the visit was more humdrum. A new and special pair of hair-brushes had been placed in the cloak-room for the King's use. I had my eye on them, but my mother, who had ideas on hygiene, said disloyally that she did not like the look of the King's bald head! They were put away, and I only acquired them 20 years later.

My grandfather was extremely hospitable, and liked nothing better than a full house. But on the day that his guests were due to leave he had a habit which disconcerted my grandmother. He would repeat in a loud voice, for the lingering offender to hear, 'I like having people to stay, but when the time comes for them to leave I wish to God they would go.' He was fastidious and would not leave the house unless he was assured of a bag of 100 brace or more.

Crawfordjohn now no longer harbours deer or boar, but it can provide wonderful sport with high pheasants, and almost everything else in the game book. It is remarkable to have kept such a reputation for some 600 years; while the neighbouring Lead Hills is one of the most consistent and prolific grouse moors in Scotland.

Douglas is 700 feet above the sea, and the shooting ground from 700 feet to 1700 feet, and it is wild. The Hirsel is 200 feet and the shooting by comparison tame. But for two miles the Tweed runs through the estate and has for long been famous for its salmon.

Tweed and Clyde rise from the same water-shed, and turn their backs to each other: the first flowing to the North Sea, the second to the Atlantic.

The Clyde might well have been as good a fishing river as the Tweed, were it not for the Falls of Clyde which drop in a series of steep and deep cascades, which no salmon could navigate. It would, too, take some courage for a salmon to swim through modern Glasgow.

But for the salmon entering the Tweed there are no such obstacles, and in the spawning season the fish can proceed in an orderly way for some sixty miles should it so desire. The Hirsel fishing is about 20 miles from the mouth at Berwick-upon-Tweed which is a convenient first resting-place for the fresh fish to lie.

The Homes were inevitably fishermen, and in the eighteenth century the Eighth Earl of Home acquired a reputation as an angler. His equipment was primitive, being a rod of 22 feet and a horse-hair line, but it was undeniably effective. In 1743 he landed a salmon of 69¾ pounds. He owned a dog which became notorious, and then famous. It would sit on the river bank at the Mill Stream opposite Wark Castle, and in a morning's fishing it would catch and land twenty or more salmon and lay them at its owner's feet. The jealous, humourless and irate owner of the South Bank of the river brought a law-suit against the dog; the case being known as 'Lord Tankerville versus a dog – the property of the Earl of Home'. Much to the joy of the Scottish side the dog won.

That monster salmon has between then and now had only one rival in the Tweed. On the Bemersyde water a fish was hooked on an autumn afternoon and when it was pitch dark with a flip of its tail it broke the gut. It was then impossible to see what had become of the salmon, but early in the morning the poachers had been busy. There on the bank they left a less than generous tail-piece, and it weighed 35 pounds!

A hundred years later the Lord Home of the day, in the month of June, averaged 14 salmon a day for six consecutive days – all of them fresh-run. By 1852 he was writing of the devastating effect of the increase of hill-drainage, and prophesying the end of the Tweed as a salmon river. He wrote to a friend – ' It is like two houses, the one covered by a roof of thatch – the other by slate. The first will drip for hours after rain – from the other it runs straight off.'

He was right in one respect. As the draining increased the summer fishing dried up, but as compensation the fish adapted themselves to run in the spring and in the autumn. His extreme pessimism was premature, for almost 100 years later on a February day three of us fishing the same stretch of water landed 64 fresh salmon in a day and – shades of Lord Tankerville – I had a retriever which landed my salmon by gripping them across the gills and delivering them to hand.

My father, true to the union of the Douglas and the Home families, inherited a love for gun and rod to which, being a skilled horseman, he added riding to hounds. In that I was not tempted to follow him, although my brother Henry did so for a short time with crippling results.

My introduction to fishing and shooting was delayed until my father returned from the First War, but to and from Gallipoli there was a regular two-way mail reporting on birds and beasts and butterflies. He would describe the hoopoes and bluethroats and the rollers, and once there was a box which had been opened and passed by the censor which contained a blown egg of a cassandra lark. So when my father was demobilized Henry and I eagerly waited for first-hand instructions in the natural history of the Borders. Wisdom dictated that we should be well-grounded before we were allowed to practise with gun or rod, and so we used to go in attendance on my father and his friends at every possible opportunity when they were shooting or fishing.

My father would demonstrate how to cast a line as straight as an arrow into the wind, or how to hold a gun relaxed but ready so as to require the minimum of movement to the shoulder.

But there was much more to it than arms drill. The distance to the first line of butts at Douglas was anything from a mile and a half upwards into the hills, and in those days we would walk every yard of it, and would make acquaintance with much wild life along the way.

The dipper would bob and curtsey ahead of us along the rocks in the stream, and as we climbed, the slim ring ousel would slip into the shadows, for it is the shyest of birds. The wheatear with its white rump would escort us, its curiosity never allowing it to let us out of its sight. The peregrine too would come diving out of the clouds, and on one occasion the duck that it struck was so close to our heads that it fell at our feet.

For some years a male bird, the tiercel, roosted on a ledge which ran round the turret of the Castle, but there was what looked to be a leather thong, jesses, attached to his leg and I think he had escaped from captivity.

So there was infinite variety. On some years when the voles had a good breeding season the hills would be alive with short-eared owls. They would sit close, and give a splendid view of their undersides, which are almost as white as their cousins' the barn owls, as they floated away light as thistledown. Nor did we waste the break for luncheon, for we would scour the heather for the apple-green caterpillars of the emperor moth, with its pink or yellow spots and black shiny spines. If there was a sedge bush near a still pool in the burn we would shake the branches for the caterpillars of the puss moth with its devilish mask and horned tail, and, if we were lucky, we could score a double as the poplar hawk moth patronized the same sedge bush.

Scotland is not a very satisfactory place for the collector of butterflies, but the mountain ringlet could be found at Douglas and the migrants could always be seen flying across the moors. When the Continent and England had been burnt up by a dry summer, the migrant clouded yellows and the painted ladies would lay their eggs, and these would hatch into butterflies in August and September, the painted ladies covering the buddleias with patches of translucent pink.

There was one extraordinary year when it was impossible to walk a yard in the heather without raising dozens of red admirals; I never discovered why it was that they took to the hills, but they were there in their millions all over the South of Scotland.

On one red-letter day in September I saw two camberwell beauties sitting on the heads of a clump of michaelmas daisies, but when I brought the family to see them they had gone.

The keeping, feeding, pupating and hatching of butterflies and moths was a hazardous but serious business for which our school authorities did not cater. My sisters did their best, but it was my father who went to the greatest lengths to see that the cycle of entomological life was not interrupted. On one occasion he sent the caterpillars of my youngest brother George to Eton in a taxi from London, rather than that they

should miss a meal of their particular food.

We would return from arduous natural history and shooting expeditions ready only for supper and bed. And if I woke at all in the night it was to a persistent hiss from the window-sill from the barn owl which lived in the Chapel Tower. It used to watch me with an unwinking eye, scornful no doubt that I could bear to waste such prolific hunting hours. And if on a moonlight night I looked on to the grass which surrounded the tower of an older Castle, there would be the ghost moths with their long, narrow and luminous white wings to add an appropriate eeriness to the scene.

Nor in terms of later life were our days in the butts wasted watching our elders shoot. We were taught never to go about with the gun cocked, but with each shot to push up the safety-catch as the gun comes to the shoulder; no time is lost by that, and no risk is run; always to unload when crossing a fence – never to swing through the line – no jealous shooting – the first barrel to be fired as far out in front as possible, and then with the gun perpendicular, and with a quick change of feet; the second shot to be taken as soon as it was safe to do so behind; and it is safe sooner than most people think, for the gun is then swinging away from the line.

Nothing is more tiresome or pointless than jealous shooting. I had two examples in my early shooting days. There was a certain colonel who shot very well, and after each drive he entered in a note book the number of cartridges which he fired against the number of birds which he killed. He had with him three dogs, and if the tally of shots to birds was not to his liking he would shamelessly send the retrievers well outside his territory.

On one occasion I saw his neighbour (who anyhow had a red face and a ready temper) clearly suffering from severe blood-pressure. He walked up to the offender and said, 'Colonel, I may not be able to shoot as well as you but I can pick up very well indeed,' and he clutched an armful of grouse and returned to his butt. Childish no doubt, but the worm turned!

The other occasion was when a young man who was a fine shot was placed up-wind of his eighty-year-old host. The former shot over forty pheasants coming down the high wind. After the drive his host came up to him and said, 'That was a marvellous exhibition, but I thought you might have left me one.' 'Oh, sir,' was the reply, 'I thought you would have missed it!'

A tendency to jealous shooting should be ruthlessly cured early in life.

As in every game involving co-ordination of eye and muscle, foot-work is the essence of success. As a guide, the left foot ought always to be pointing towards the shooter's target. These basic rules and much more we learnt by observation on the moors.

Standing with the guns at The Hirsel brought an entirely fresh lot of birds to our notice. In winter the branches of the larches would be full of the twittering of the long-tailed tits, still in their large families, but finding comfort and security from the cold in travelling in packs. The golden crested wrens – the most vulnerable of all the small birds to ice and snow, combing the needles and cones of the fir trees for the hibernating insects on which they must live until the spring, and occasionally, when the frost was keen, the crossbills would come to the tops of the tall Scots firs.

From the reedy fringes of the lake, after an easterly gale, all the wildfowl from the shores of the North Sea would join the permanent residents – the mallard and the teal, the shoveller and tufted – the high-light being the arrival of the smew. That furtive little bird, the water rail, would always be there, and once I unexpectedly ran right into a bittern standing like a statue frozen to the swamp.

Fishing is a quiet sport, and birds and animals will approach unafraid. Oyster-catchers and ringed plovers would come within a few yards, and one day, so realistic was my salmon-fly, that I hooked a tern.

Sometimes as the packs of grouse flew over the butts, or the pheasants crossed the high valley, Henry and I would dream of the day when we might graduate to a proper shoot. But for the time being our ambitions were limited. How modest was well illustrated by the first entry in my brother George's game book. 'Rabbits 1. Comment – shot very well.'

But even if one thought in single figures there was a wealth of excitement to be had at Douglas for the beginner, for the varieties of game were many.

Grouse, black game, pheasant, partridge, woodcock, snipe, golden plover, mallard, teal, several species of wildfowl, geese, pigeons, hares and rabbits.

Our goal was in one day to get the lot, but that could not be done in the summer holidays as the pheasant was not in season, nor had the wild geese arrived; but any one of that list was a prize.

I must now say my first and last word about 'blood-sports'. To shoot or not to shoot is a matter for the individual decision, but the following is worth careful consideration in the balance of argument.

The earliest entries in the Douglas game book of the 1880s referred to a Colonel Pye and servant who used to walk for grouse on the hills. An average day for them was three birds. At that time over an area of moorland roughly comparable to that of today the grouse population must have varied between a few hundreds and a thousand. There followed control of vermin and conservation of heather, so that over the years the grouse population multiplied many times. I calculate that now in a bad year there will be about 2000 grouse on the Douglas moors, and on a good year twelve to fifteen thousand.

So although more grouse are shot than in the days of Colonel Pye there are many more alive.

No party of guns, however expert, will account for more than half of the birds on a given moor. The bags at Douglas over the last fifty years have ranged between eight hundred and ten thousand grouse. The sportsman, therefore, while he kills game-birds, can properly claim to be a conserver, for the numbers of the main species of game-birds have increased ten-fold. I do not know about the 'morality' of shooting and fishing; but I take hope from the last words of a splendid sportsman and devout Christian to his priest and confessor. 'Father,' he asked, 'will there be shooting and fishing in Heaven?'

Thus my apprenticeship to nature started, and the pursuit of it has remained a constant joy.

Even in the Foreign Office I could set my watch by the evening flight of the ducks from St James's Park – over the Horse Guards Parade to the Thames estuary – and select a right and left with my imaginary gun.

One of Henry's days when he was alone illustrates the kind of bag which could come our way if luck was on our side.

Grouse	3	Woodcock	1
Black game	2	Mallard	1
Partridge	12	Teal	1
Pheasants	5	Pigeon	1
Golden plover	2	Hare	1
Snipe	4	Rabbits	2

That is 'hunting' at its best.

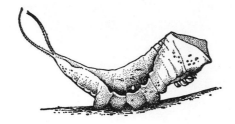

CHAPTER II

The Grouse

Each sportsman will have his favourite game-bird. Mine is the red grouse. I will give my reasons. It is totally wild; the mountain and moorland scenery in which the grouse lives is beautiful, romantic and often spectacular, while the challenge presented to the shooter is incomparable.

The partridge will explode over a belt of trees like a firework; the high pheasant, planing in the open sky with his wings still, sets a problem in ballistics; the woodcock will turn and twist; the snipe will jink; and the ducks and teal will dive and swerve, but for sheer strength of flight and aerobatics the grouse is the champion all-rounder.

The cock bird is proud and possessive, and in his full plumage with the blood-red streak above the eye he looks it, and acts accordingly. Having chosen his nesting site he will defend it against all comers; indeed so tenacious is he that if, by some blight of nature the food supply around his castle is decimated, he will stay and die rather than move. There are even many authenticated tales of attacks on human beings who have strayed on to his preserve.

When the grouse nest at the end of April and early May the weather is often rough and cold, and nature has wisely provided a more than usually chalky shell to their eggs to assist survival in the late April frosts.

The population is assisted by the fact that both cock and hen are attentive parents; should one of the brood fall into a drain as often happens, both will pilot the chick along until a way out can be found.

Even on a moor which is well-keepered there are plenty of enemies. The carrion crow will hunt every tuft of heather for eggs, and the stoats are always busy. I once shot a grouse coming down a gale of wind and it fell about fifty yards behind me. When I went to pick it up there was a weasel with its claws embedded in the grouse's neck and both bird and beast had a pellet through the head. It had clearly pounced at the moment of take-off, and clung for dear life as the grouse sped down the wind. Its luck was not in. The peregrine falcon will take some grouse, and I have seen the low-flying hen harrier clear a grouse drive.

But by far the worst of the vermin is the fox. It will prefer a rabbit or a number of voles, but on the mountains there is virtually nothing but the blue hare which is skinny and un-appetizing, so the foxes go for the grouse. A dog fox and his vixen, when feeding their cubs, become mass murderers. I remember finding forty carcasses of grouse at the mouth of one fox-earth, and the two of them had only been in residence for a matter of days.

The deadliest of the killers is the epidemic disease. The strongyle worm is present in every bird when in good health, but when there is a combination of frosted heather and a large number of grouse, it takes advantage of the low physical condition of the birds to multiply exceedingly, and then to infect and kill. The first signs of disease usually appear in the last half of April when the cocks will die first, to be followed by a large percentage of the population of the moor.

Management of the heather, and a proper rotation of the plant by burning, can do something to modify the incidence of the disease, for over 90 per cent of the food of the grouse is heather at all times of year, so that a plentiful supply at the best ages for feeding is clearly beneficial; so too is grit, as the natural supply – now that even minor roads are tarred – never seems to be quite enough. But however much care is taken there will come years when the grouse multiply too fast and the bloom on the heather is poor and the plants frosted, and then the dead birds can be picked up by the cartload. Once the pestilence has struck, the grouse moor is a desolate place and recovery is slow.

Another pest which can decimate a moor is the heather-beetle. It is a coppery colour and flies in May and June, but it is the grub which causes the trouble as it eats the roots and young shoots of the heather. The first sign is that the moor turns a russet brown. There is no cure, as spraying would be on too large a scale. Burning helps a quick recovery on hard dry ground, but on a wet moor, unless great care is taken, the grass will beat the heather.

The ideal pattern for burning is a rotation of one-fifteenth of the heather area each year. But that is easier said than done. At Douglas, for example, half the moors are wet even where the drainage is good, and half are much drier.

On the latter, following muir-burn, the green shoots of the young heather will be seen in the second year, but in the wetter ground it will be five or seven years before any fresh growth appears. Care has to be taken in such areas, as over-burning can result in tussocky grass becoming the permanent crop.

For the thirty years which followed the pioneering of Colonel Pye, the shooting at Douglas was over dogs. The sleek

setters and pointers were beautifully trained, and with every muscle taut and tails as stiff as ramrods, they stalked up to the grouse which lay in the thick heather. With the handler encouraging the pointing dogs, and with the young shooter quivering almost as much as the dog, the moment was one of high anticipation. The temptation to the beginner, when the grouse burst out of cover, is to fire almost at random in the general direction of the covey, when what is wanted is discipline and cool deliberate selection. Even after years of practice the pulse will still race.

There is a lot to be said for shooting over dogs. Early in the season the old birds in the covey will be the first to rise, and a high percentage of them will be shot, which ensures a breeding stock which will in the main be young. The pointer ranging the hill and suddenly coming to a frozen halt is a satisfying sight, and the handling of the dogs needs real skill. The only disadvantage when compared with other ways of shooting grouse is that the shots lack variety. The birds will usually be flying away from the gun, which is the least interesting of the targets which can be presented.

At Douglas the problem of method solved itself, for as sheep-farming became more intensive the heather became shorter and the grouse wilder. With some reluctance the pointer and setter were discarded, and first walking in line and then driving to the butts took over. There is a lot of satisfaction to be had from walking grouse, particularly if they are pushed into the wind; wherever possible that should be the rule, for the further they are taken from their home-ground the more they will break back down the wind and provide a rich variety of shots to the guns.

The walk is the more exciting on the steep slopes where accuracy will depend on the shooter keeping his balance among rocks and long and slippery heather.

There is all the difference between that and the flat floor of the shooting school. The simple guide to the beginner (although by no means easy in practice) is to give most of his attention to his feet. To try and shoot with the hips turning but the feet static is to invite disaster, while success will surely follow when the left foot is pointed towards the bird and the balance is even and firm.

One more tip can be given. Nine out of ten misses will result from shooting behind and below the bird. Theoretically it is possible to shoot in front of a grouse, but the occasions are so rare that for practical purposes they can be ignored.

I have greatly enjoyed both shooting over dogs and walking in line, but I am bound to give pride of place to the grouse drive. That it is an art is not too high a claim.

The aim, given a wide space of moorland, is to collect the birds into a settling area and then, using the elements of contour, wind and the skill of beaters and game-keepers, to coax them over the guns which occupy butts on a front of some three hundred yards. That is not a very large stretch when seen on the mountainside. The ideal is to drive the coveys off their habitual living- and feeding-ground down the wind. If that can be done two or three times then the fully feathered birds will have every incentive to fly home, even if it is up-wind and against a stiff gale.

Given virgin ground with no existing butts to distract the eye, the owner of a moor and his head game-keeper have only one infallible guide. The grouse by nature will always fly along

the contour of the hill. The moor therefore which has well-defined rounded hills is the easiest to drive and to butt. The line of guns can be sited at a convenient distance behind a ridge, and will be virtually invisible, while the grouse will not fly too far once they have gone behind the butts as they will be quickly out of sight and sound.

On many moors the features are by no means clear-cut, and it is here that the placing of the butts requires real skill, and the control of the flight of the grouse is an art. In such cases the only way to success is instinct, observation and trial and error.

There is one way in which the game-keeper can help the guns. The bottoms of the butts should be flat and dry, and the whole large enough for the shooter to lower his gun and re-load without hitting the walls.

In the early days of grouse-driving the pioneers contrived their lines of butts for the prevailing wind only, and they were very good at it. But the ingenious owner will try and build butts which can be used in all sorts of winds, and when that is successfully achieved the prospect of good sport and more shooting days is greatly enhanced.

It is on the comparatively flat or undulating ground that the skill of drivers and flankers will be really tested. There the grouse have to be guided, sidled, and nudged into the catch-ment area, and then, with exact timing, the main line of beaters must straighten and advance and propel the birds over the line of guns. Timing is the essence of the matter.

The beaters having played their part, the skilled flanker can make a great deal of difference to the size of the bag. The secret of good flanking of birds which aim to fly out at the sides, is to turn the heads of the grouse which are leading the covey or the pack in the right direction. The secret is surprise and timing. There is a fleeting moment which has to be recognized when a flanker can rise from the heather, and with one or two deft strokes of his flag, achieve the change in flight which will send the birds on the right course. When the heads are turned, the flagging should cease. That too is the mark of the really good flanker. The menace is one who, zealous but ignorant, will wave at everything within sight; he can easily ruin a good drive.

When the wind is near to a gale and the grouse are being driven into it, a flanker who knows his business will place himself level with if not behind the line of butts. When he raises his flag even a little the grouse will slide down the line of guns, giving several of them good shooting before they resume the direction of their flight.

On one or two occasions early in the season, when the flight of birds is not so strong, and when we were shooting in a gale, I remember my father organizing an up-wind drive with the guns as onlookers. Had the grouse been shot at while tacking against such a wind the majority would probably have been carried away back over the beaters' heads, and been lost for the rest of the shoot. It takes some nerve with sceptical and impatient guests looking on, but the ruse can sometimes pay a handsome dividend.

I can recall one day in particular when we took the risk in order to get the grouse into an area where we hoped to deal with them in the shelter 'under the wind'. After the first two drives we had 3c brace and after the next two 180 brace. It had paid to gamble.

I have described another day when Edward VII was shooting and the grouse came home on their own. The King had brought with him a Russian Count who was accustomed to shooting bears, but had never been in a grouse butt. For safety he was put at the end of the line. During the drive pack after pack of black game flew past him and he never fired his gun. Asked by the King the reason for his restraint, he replied, 'I thought they were the poultry from the farm over there.'

My father could not bear the sight of a party of guns mooning about the house with nothing to do, so everyone was ruthlessly sent out to the shoot whatever the weather conditions. On the bigger shoots each gun was attended by his valet-cum-loader. There was one of these in particular who had the well-deserved reputation of looking after himself first and last and inside and out. On one day the rain was bucketing down, and there, sure enough, was Mr Simpson completely protected – leggings, mackintosh, sou'wester and all, enquiring of the world in general, ' 'as anybody seen Lord 'enry's coat?' His master was long ago soaked to the skin.

Weather has always been a trial to the host and hostess of a shooting-party. It is said that a guest of Sir Timothy Eden's, who was early down to breakfast, found him at the dining-room window shaking his fist at the pouring rain and saying, 'Oh God, how like you!' I know the feeling well.

The older generation, who shot before the First World War, had the advantage of constant practice at a wide variety of game, with the result that they were hard to beat for speed and accuracy. The Lord Elphinstone of that time was such a one, and I only once saw him knocked off his rhythm. A covey of eight grouse came towards him, and due to some freak of flight, he killed seven with his first barrel; he was so astonished that the survivor went unscathed.

For the beginner there is one rule which is absolute. Always subject to safety, shoot at grouse in front of the butts. The actual shot is much easier, and much more satisfying than one at a bird bumming away behind. It is also unselfish as it splits the covey, and gives to the guns on either side the chance of a shot they would not otherwise have. For some psychological reason it is difficult to persuade oneself to fire far out in front, but it is the infallible mark of the good shot. It is of course common sense for it is possible to shoot a bird behind at a distance of thirty yards – how much easier it must be if the grouse is flying into the pattern of shot.

The grouse is the master of the elements, whether coming down the wind like a bullet, or tacking into it and yet covering the ground with deceptive speed. It might be supposed that the 'slow' grouse up-wind would be the easier to shoot, and yet I have seen good shots almost totally humiliated by birds which look so slow and pass so close that it seemed they could be caught in a butterfly net. I think that the reason for the poor shooting is that no two grouse are travelling at the same pace, as they hover and drop and rise while trying to cheat the wind.

When driving grouse the host should always remember the beaters. They are not to be pitied, for walking light on the hill is a healthy pursuit. But they would always prefer to start early rather than finish late. Nor should a host, however well he knows the line of butts, try and move a guest into a butt different from that which he has drawn in order to get him a better drive. My father used to do this, and almost invariably the grouse ignored the favoured guest and patronized the Home brothers.

As with any other game involving co-ordination of eye and muscle, practice helps a lot. When coveys and packs are advancing in quick succession it is possible for the shooter to choose his favourite angle for shooting without worrying about the more difficult birds. All the same the most valuable man at a shoot is he who has few chances and takes them.

I have seen grouse-driving days which produced very large bags, but I missed the biggest of all.

On the 16th of August I broke my right thumb while playing cricket, and was therefore prevented from shooting on the famous Shipka Pass at Wermergill in Yorkshire. The bag on August 18th was 2697 grouse.

In October on the same ground, numbers and quality were combined for even in snow and wind we averaged 200 brace a day for five days.

There are few things so exhilarating as to be on a grouse-moor on an autumn morning when the sun begins to dispel the mist. On all sides the grouse call of 'go-back' comes echoing down from the hills. So for me, of all the game-birds, the grouse is King.

CHAPTER III

The Blackcock

If I omit the capercailzie, as I must for it does not live south of the Firths of Forth and Clyde, then the blackcock is the majestic heavy-weight of the moorland game-birds.

There is no more spectacular display in the bird world than the cocks collected at their mating dance in the spring, when at their 'lek' they strut and bow and posture with their tail-feathers erect and stretched to a full half-circle.

It must be said that his wife – the grey hen – scarcely

deserves this elaborate celebration of courtship. Perhaps it is her protest against polygamy, but she is dowdy, soft in the head and a bad mother; she will set off with her chicks in the rushy country which is their habitat, and she will push right ahead – feeding herself, with never a backward glance at the stragglers in her brood. The result is that mortality among black game is high.

In theory, with the large increase in forests planted by the Forestry Commission, the numbers ought to increase, but the forester doesn't approve of the blackcock which sits on the tender leaders of his young trees, while so far the grey hen has not found a way to carry her young over the wire with which the woods are so often netted.

Whether from pity, or from a genuine belief that to spare the hens would increase the species, neither my grandfather nor my father would allow a grey hen to be shot; even a mistake had a frosty reception.

In the early part of the century black game had been very numerous on the Lanarkshire/Dumfries border. In one day at Drumlanrig in 1875, 105 blackcock and 120 grouse were shot; and in 1880 99 blackcock and 153 grouse. The bulk of the 1880 bag was achieved in the morning, the poor afternoon being attributed to the gaudy ostrich feathers in the hat of one of the Victorian ladies which diverted any bird approaching the line of guns.

Some idea of the numbers at Douglas is given by the fact that the Lord Elphinstone, of whose prowess I have written earlier, was able to fire twenty-two shots, and that with one gun, before a pack of black game passed by.

At present the opening date for the shooting of black game

is 20 August. That is wrong, for the old birds are moulting and undignified without their tails, and the young ones are still unfledged. The date should be changed to mid-September by which time the birds are fair game.

At that time of year the old cocks used to reveal an Achilles heel. When, in a wet season, the stooks of oats were standing late in the fields, the blackcock would gorge upon the wet corn. I have seen them so drunk that they would wobble off their perch quite unable to fly. Today the modern harvester sweeps the fields clean, but in those days the poachers would sit in the stooks and pull the cocks down by their legs. I never saw an intoxicated hen!

In an early and wet autumn it was sometimes impossible to keep the grouse and black game off the farmer's corn. I remember leaving Henry in a field one afternoon to collect a few grouse for the house. When I returned after two hours he had 40 brace and some blackcock. He was not popular as it was a bad year.

With the sparing of the grey hens, there was nevertheless a continuing drop in numbers of the species, and as the environment was largely unchanged we concluded that this must be cause and effect. We therefore started selective shooting of hens. From late August until mid-October the old hen is fairly easily recognizable and it was them that we made our target. After three or four seasons it was apparent that we were on to something as the numbers visibly increased. Our hunch had been right. These old barren and jealous ladies had been tyrannizing the young and preventing them from mating.

The blackcock, once he has grown his feathers, is vigilant and cunning. It is possible to stalk him, but much more often

than not he will fly off when just out of range.

One such attempt had an unusual end. A young friend of Henry's during a long morning had insisted on carrying with him a bottle of Burgundy, and when it came to lunch on the hill he drank the whole of it. Immediately afterwards eight blackcock were spied and the crawl began. Henry as guide was some 40 yards ahead when there was an explosion – a loud shout of rage, and a flurry of blackcock. Henry's friend in his exhilaration had been worming his way along, with the gun at full cock, and caught the trigger in the heather, peppering Henry in the behind. I noticed that this visitor never returned to shoot at Douglas.

But if they are masters at evading the stalker, the blackcock has one habit which can be exploited. They tend, when disturbed, to follow the same route from one place to another, and careful reconnaissance will often reveal some land-mark on the way which has caught their eye. It may be a single tree or the prominent corner of a wall on the hill-side by which they take their bearings in an otherwise empty and featureless landscape. They will tend to follow that line several times until the accurate placing of guns has taken its toll and made them shy of it.

By and large the rule with game-birds is that the larger the bird the faster it flies. The capercailzie is proof of that, for its wing-beat is silent and it looks to be slow, but it is in fact exceedingly fast.

So it is with the blackcock. The slow and regular rhythm of its wings is entirely deceptive, until black game fly alongside grouse, when they are seen to outpace them every time. Until the beginner has had a string of misses he will never believe that they are travelling at such a speed, and it is long odds on the bird.

I remember two days in particular in which black game featured prominently. We shot pheasants in the morning, and then went for two drives on the heather, which was all the short November afternoon would allow.

My game book in 1926 reads:

November 23rd	Grouse	80	
	Black game	53	
	Pheasants	41	
	Partridges	2	plus 'various'
November 24th	Grouse	54	
	Black game	41	
	Pheasants	42	plus 'various'

I can recall to this day every detail of those drives in the setting sun, which turned the heather as black as the cocks themselves.

Then and always we were six guns or less as my father wisely insisted that more were a mob, and got in each other's way. He held that there should be a law to say so.

Black game will never recover their numbers to the point of fifty years ago, nor will there be enough to keep the Kings Own Scottish Borderers in tail-feathers, but if the opening date is delayed, and the old hens are not allowed to boss the young, there will be plenty to provide one of the loveliest sights in the autumn which is black game sitting in birch-trees when the ground is covered in snow.

CHAPTER IV

The Pheasant

The cock pheasant in all his flamboyant finery can claim to be the most spectacular of the British birds. Not that he is a native of the country, for pheasants had their origin in the bogs and swamps of Asia Minor and further east. They came to Britain with the Romans. They still prefer the marshes, and it is only the foxes which have driven them to roost in the trees and become a bird of the woods.

At Douglas, which isn't a hunting country and the fox is never hunted, the pheasants spend their nights in the rushes by choice, and they are as often as not driven from the rough hill-sides.

A few years ago, motoring from Peking to the Great Wall of China, I saw pheasants flying from the paddy and rice-fields into the swamps which were their original habitat.

That they were wise to roost in the trees in Britain was well illustrated by my brother Henry's experiment with wild turkeys. He bought two dozen pairs and distributed them in congenial places at The Hirsel. But nothing would persuade them to roost in the trees, and all were snapped up by the foxes in the first season.

If the pheasant is under-estimated in this country as a game-bird it may be because so many are reared that it has become one of our commonest birds, and because when there are too many hatched and fed on unsuitable ground, the shoot can become artificial and unworthy of a splendid sporting bird.

When the pheasants are driven in flat country from one wood to another close by, and the majority fly low, interest can wane and the birds are only missed because the shooter has become lazy.

But use ingenuity to produce the pheasant where it ought to be – high in the sky – and the same bird can present the highest test of skill. In fact I would name the most difficult of all the shots to be the cock pheasant which rises far off and gains maximum height as he approaches the line of guns and then, setting his wings, glides to his destination far behind. There is nothing but the bare sky by which to measure his pace, no means to tell whether he is sliding side-ways or dropping – in short he is the shooter's nightmare.

Various gimmicks have been recommended to encompass

[45]

such a pheasant's downfall, one of which is for the shooter to keep his eyes on the ground until the very last moment before the bird is all but vertical overhead. The idea is right, for to poke and hang on is fatal, but the flesh is weak, and the temptation to watch the aerobatics irresistible. Anyhow these are the pheasants which most often win, and they richly deserve to do so, for they show daring, defiance and guile in high degree.

I have heard many an argument about the size of shot which will give the highest average of success at the really high pheasants. No. 8 has it on pattern, and no. 5 on hitting power on impact. The argument is still unresolved, and the answer is that it doesn't matter if the pheasant is hit in the neck. I settle for no. 6 as a compromise and a good answer for everything all round the season.

I once saw the French Ambassador in London, who shot very well, achieve a right and left at pheasants the placing of which must be unique. He was standing in a steep valley about 300 yards from our house at Douglas. His first high pheasant landed stone dead on the front door-step, while the second crashed through the pantry window where the man who was washing-up found it literally on his plate!

Many owners of pheasant shoots, particularly the syndicates where a head-keeper has the biggest say in the nature of the drives, settle too easily for the low pheasant. Naturally the keeper wants to see a high percentage of the birds for which he has been responsible killed, so he will as a rule go for quantity rather than quality. On that the host should never allow himself to be soft-hearted.

It is true that sometimes in flat country there seems to be no alternative to the conventional way of driving the pheasants from wood to wood with the guns standing some seventy yards back from the coverts. But even then with the exercise of a little ingenuity much more satisfying results can be achieved.

If the pheasants are fed in root fields or hedgerows at a distance outside the wood, and driven back into it with the guns entirely visible in their path, the birds will fly higher and faster.

Even better results can be had from root fields adjacent to a wood if host and head-keeper have the nerve to walk the pheasants away from the covert with the guns a hundred yards behind the advancing line. The pheasants will then fly to the wood in which they roost and will gain height and curl and present very interesting shots.

When planning a pheasant shoot from scratch, and planting new woods, it is often assumed that the pheasants will fly highest from a wood on the hill to one on a lower level. But that often results in the pheasants dipping and the best results are usually to be had if the pheasants are aimed at a covert rather above the height of that from which they are flushed.

A wind too, will improve almost any shoot, although in a gale the cock pheasant finds it very undignified to have his long tail blown over his head and his steering totally upset.

If there is one thing more than another which a host and his keeper should remember about a pheasant it is that it runs. The organizer of a shoot therefore can positively run the birds to the destination which will serve the drive which he plans, while negatively he must stop them from running along the various escape routes which offer themselves along the way.

A good shoot can always be spotted by the efficiency of the

placing of the 'stops'. As a rule it is better to have fewer beaters and more stops than the other way round. Once the gaps have been blocked the pheasants will run far further than the average keeper can bring himself to admit.

There is however, one condition for success – it is Quiet. The only noise allowed should be the tapping of the sticks of the beaters. Like the snipe, there is nothing a pheasant dislikes so much as the human voice. A gun-shot will have far less effect on the pheasant which is running ahead, so back guns can safely be part of such a manoeuvre. When there is shouting the pheasants will panic and squat and go back or fly out at the sides, but with the tap-tap-tap, and a slow advance the birds will run ahead picking at this or that nourishment on the way and not unduly alarmed. They can be kept going steadily away from home until the covert is reached which has been chosen for the rise over the guns.

Lord Leicester, at Holkham Hall in Norfolk, was a famous exponent and practitioner of the art of showing pheasants, and a dramatic illustration of it was when, from a long way, the birds were 'tapped' into a famous stand which was named the Scarbrough Clump. For over an hour in the afternoon the pheasants would fly back the way they had come and very high.

There was a story of his riposte to his keeper who had pro- tested that to run the pheasants to a certain destination was impossible. 'If you know how to do it you can run them into my front door' was all the change he got!

There is another famous shoot on the banks of the River Wear in County Durham where one aspect of the skill of showing pheasants is regularly demonstrated. There the birds cannot be anything but high as they cross from one wood to another over a steep and narrow valley, but there are many thousands of them in a confined area and the problem is to flush them in small numbers so that over a longish time the shooters can have the best chance of making a good bag. I recall one day when eight guns shot over 3000 pheasants, and I do not think that I ever saw more than thirty to forty in the air at one time, and they were always well spread. That represents total mastery of the art of showing the birds to the best advantage.

In such ways the time of each stand can be greatly extended and the spectacle, the excitement and the challenge enormously enhanced. These techniques do not only apply to the large battue for they will improve any shoot however modest.

In these circumstances the well-run pheasant shoot on a clear winter's day is a spectacular sight and an entirely pleasurable experience. Everything is designed so that the pheasants fly high, which is itself a compliment to a fine game-bird.

Steady rain, with no wind, is the bane of the pheasant shooter. The birds with their feathers soaked can scarcely rise let alone gain height. If the host has to proceed, and it is not easy to cancel guns when it is still dark at 8 o'clock, it is a kindness to the beaters to leave until last the young plantations where the rain-drops hang until late in the day.

Luncheon when shooting always presents a problem. During the interval grouse which have been collected will go back home and so will the partridges, but with the pheasant the difficulty is the shortage of daylight hours. Some hosts organize a snack at eleven and luncheon at three o'clock; the trouble then is that the snack is too early and the meal too late. During the last hour of such a programme the shooters inevitably get tired. I prefer luncheon at one o'clock, but the host must be ruthless in chasing the guests out again into the field.

So far I have written of the set-piece which will apply to any shoot of a hundred pheasants or more. But perhaps the greatest enjoyment is to be had from the 'cocks only' shoot at the tail-end of the season, or from the hunt of the hedgerows by a couple of guns and a dog.

The key to success in the first case is to drive the woods in a way which the wily cock pheasant will not expect. In the hedgerow a lot depends on the steadiness of the dog and on the gun's ability to place himself so that he can deal with birds which will often go back. In either case it becomes a battle of wits in which as often as not victory will go to the old cock with the crooked mind, the fleetest foot and the longest spur.

CHAPTER V

The Partridge

If ever there was an advertisement for plump domesticity it is the partridge. It is well-deserved for they are monogamous, and a pair, given reasonable conditions in the mating season, will produce large families well into the 'teens, and they will look after their young with fussy and businesslike efficiency. In that they show up the polygamists like the blackcock and the pheasant.

On a shooting day this modest bird is a different being, endowed with such skills that it has few rivals at testing the sportsman's eye and ability. Drive a covey over a belt of trees behind which are the guns, and it will explode like shrapnel, scattering in all directions. At that moment the self-control of the shooter is in danger of disintegration. But although unnerved, he has one advantage. The partridge, being smaller than the grouse, is slower in flight, and there is time for recovery.

The theory of partridge-driving is essentially the same as that for grouse, but the concept is more tactical than strategic, the scale of operation being as a chess-board to a lawn tennis court.

That is quite an apt analogy, for if the squares represent fields, and there are three or four of stubble and grass to each root field, then the tactics are to move the partridges from the former into the latter, and then drive them from one field of cover into another.

The pattern of farming is seldom ideal for the organizer of a shoot, but the essence of the plan will be to use the thick root-crops in the hope that the coveys will be broken up and thus give the guns the best chance to make a bag.

East Anglia, which has the light soil in which the partridges revel, was the area of England where driving was developed to the finest art and the precision of manoeuvre reached which is required if the partridges are to be held in a comparatively small area of ground for the whole day. Hedges were kept high, and belts of Scots fir planted over which the partridges were 'lifted' so that the shooting was clean and fast.

Sometimes the birds could be driven over a belt of beech trees, fifty or sixty feet in height, and on a golden October day that was the champagne of shooting.

But curiously enough it was in East Lothian in Scotland that

[53]

I saw a day's driving work out to total satisfaction. I had seen the plan of campaign on the evening before the shoot. There were four fields of corn stubble or grass to one turnip or potato field. The pattern was repeated four times in the area which was to be shot. To make the best of the day we required a west wind to carry the birds by stages down to the catchment area of gorse and broom which lay along the top of the cliffs of the Firth of Forth and which would comprise the final drive.

In the morning the wind was west all right, but it was a full gale, and in it the partridges looked like sparrows. As there were so many we proceeded with the plan. At 3.30 in the afternoon we had 50 brace with one drive to go. In that final stand of the day we added 98 brace to the score; the birds, being determined to reach their habitual roosting ground before dark, flew without hesitation into the teeth of the gale. It was a spectacular example of the use of the wind to fill a cul-de-sac, but it took some nerve to shoot at all in a near hurricane.

Flanking can play some part in driving partridges, but it is not nearly so effective as in grouse-driving, for once the partridge heads the wrong way nothing will turn it.

All my life I have done my best to avoid walking-up partridges in turnip fields, except over the verges of the arable fields and the moors where the plots are smaller and the crop is not so thick. In turnips or kale the shot to the walking guns is usually uninteresting, and the picking-up of runners is distracting and time-wasting to dogs and all concerned. A trick for a knowing gun is to place himself down-wind at the end of the line.

Of all the game-birds the partridge is the one which has suffered most from the adoption of scientific methods of agriculture. They like to live on weeds and insects, and both are rightly anathema to the modern farmer. The sprays – the making of silage in early summer – the ploughing of the stubble almost as soon as the corn is reaped – the destruction of hedges – all contribute to the reduced numbers.

The partridge, nesting as it does in the grass of the hedge-row, or in rough places, is very vulnerable to vermin. The fox parades up the hedges, while the innocent-looking hedgehog will snuffle along, turn the nest inside out, and suck the eggs on the spot. The most ingenious deterrent which I ever saw was a trap in hunting country where the fox was never shot. When touched by the predator it delivered a sharp blow to the jaw. It was always placed within a yard of the nest, and the partridges seemed to know that it was there for their protection as the nest was hardly ever deserted.

The French partridge seems to cope with these agricultural disabilities more successfully than his English relative, but it is a poor substitute as it runs rather than flies, and flies predictably straight.

Nevertheless, though the bags of the early part of the century will never be repeated, even in the best of the partridge

country, the sun can still work wonders. In the dry summers of 1975 and 1976 there were large coveys everywhere, and plenty of partridges to drive.

Partridges are easy to rear, but in the first shooting season they are apt to pack, and during the following winter they largely disappear. The reason is all too clear; there simply is not, under modern conditions of clean stubbles, and early ploughing, the food supply to keep them alive. So we must hope that fine summers will come at intervals which are not too long. Good keeping can help a lot, but it is the sun which guarantees success.

I must place the partridge second only to the grouse in the sportsman's catalogue of birds which test his all-round skill, and which give him the greatest pleasure and delight.

CHAPTER VI

The Woodcock

The woodcock is the most solitary of the game-birds, and also the most elusive, and the shooter, apart from knowing where to hunt, must first discover whether the woodcock are 'in'. That jargon derives from the fact that those birds which breed in Britain are apt to move off to the south and west towards the end of September, and the bulk of those which are shot arrive from Scandinavia, Russia and Eastern Europe with the November moon. I have seen them dropping in on the coast of East Lothian, singly or in twos or threes, so exhausted on landing that they can scarcely fly.

When I was a boy it was comparatively rare to find the

woodcock nesting in the South of Scotland; now, both at The Hirsel and at Douglas, they do so by the score. When she is on her nest the hen sits extraordinarily tight. There was lately one at Hirsel in a rhododendron wood which is open to the public. I suppose a thousand people passed within two yards of her while she sat, and she never so much as batted an eyelid. We debated whether to indicate that the nest was there, but we decided to trust to her protective colouring and her courage to sit it out without being seen. She vindicated our judgment.

The woodcock's eye is large and unblinking, and so set that it has a range of sight of 360° – the only blind spot is in front of its nose.

Woodcock are early nesters, and by May the young are flying well. There is no pleasanter sight on a May evening than to see the woodcock 'roding' in acrobatic flight, all the time emitting low grunts of satisfaction at their own performance. They will follow a flight path with faithful regularity.

For a long time there was controversy as to whether or not the woodcock carried its young. The answer is a definite 'yes'. I have several times seen them flopping away with a chick gripped between the thighs, and once with chicks on the mother's back.

To obtain proof Henry and I surrounded a nest, which was due to hatch, with high wire with a very small mesh. By the next day the young had been carried to a distance outside the enclosure.

A reliable observer also once told me that she had seen a woodcock carry a chick across the River Findhorn and then return to ferry another.

The woodcock migration is fairly constant in numbers,

unless a flight meets too strong a wind, when considerable numbers will drown in the North Sea, or when there is a long spell of frost, when they will be found sitting beside the frozen springs, too weak to move. Then the breeding stock suffers and recovery will take two years or more.

Some woodcock are light-coloured and others dark, and on a day's shooting the number of each kind will be about equal. Some hold that the dark birds are the migrants from Scandinavia, but I am inclined to think that it is a characteristic of the individual bird, as I have seen both varieties at all times of year.

However that may be, the fact that they are here today and gone tomorrow adds to the excitement of the shoot which, unless it is organized when the birds are 'in', will often result in disappointment. The weather regulates their movements and there is little doubt that they can anticipate an unfavourable change.

A year or two ago, on the east end of the Lammermuirs, the woodcock were reported to be 'in' and in large numbers. We arranged a shoot for two days ahead. On the chosen morning the conditions were apparently exactly the same as before, but the barometer was beginning to fall very steeply. There was not a woodcock to be seen. That night there was a freak fall of eighteen inches of snow.

The weather will largely decide the size of the bag of woodcock in any given season. When the weather is hard they will concentrate on the feeding grounds which stay open and so are more easily found and shown.

The habit of the woodcock is to sleep in the cover of bracken or juniper or young trees by day and to feed in the bogs at night. If the presence of cows has brought up a plentiful supply of worms then the birds are in paradise. The key to the presence of the woodcock is the earth-worm, and then the right form of shelter. The ideal conditions for wood-cock are provided by young larch coverts which let in the sun-light, and have a clear floor on which the birds can run about. Yews and gorse, hollies and rhododendrons, until they become too overgrown and tangled, will fulfil the same functions. At all times the birds like quiet.

The woodcock is a very acceptable addition to the pheasant shoot, but it is only very exceptionally that a good bag is made on such days. The best results are had either by two guns hunt-ing the likely haunts with a few beaters and some spaniels, or by four guns on a day of mixed walking and driving.

When the woodcock are driven the placing of the guns is of absolute importance. The forward guns must not stand too far back from the covert, for the woodcock on coming out into the open is as likely as not to turn straight back over the tops of the trees. Then as many woodcock will fly out at the sides as will go forward. Two walking guns – one on each side – will have as many chances as those which are ahead, and it will pay every time for these two to halt some twenty yards from the corner of the wood which is being driven, for invariably towards the end woodcock will emerge too low for the for-ward guns to shoot at them safely, and they will flip back along the edge of the trees.

The woodcock seems to delight in teasing the shooter by diving straight at his neighbour or at the beaters. The gun therefore who has the instinct to get himself in the best position to shoot with safety in as many directions as possible, is an invaluable member of the team.

The woodcock plays every possible trick of twist and turn, but it cannot help giving one aid to the hunter. When the bird rises it gives an audible 'flip' as it jet-propels itself from the ground. To the 'flip' the shooter's ear is acutely attuned, for when the cover is thick the sound gives him the cue to turn in the direction from which the bird is most likely to appear, and a useful second is gained.

The essentially solitary nature of the woodcock was dramatically illustrated during one shoot on the island of Islay. In nine days many hundreds of woodcock were shot; there was only one right and left achieved, and one other opportunity which was barely a chance.

I can recall only one day in my life when I thought that it was too cold to shoot. There was a howling northerly gale and the thermometer hung around zero, but the woodcock were 'in'. The cold snap had been sudden, and the ice-crust on the bogs was thin, so that our feet by lunch-time were in danger of frost-bite. Somebody suggested pouring whisky into our boots. It says much for the value of money in the 1920s that about five shillings' worth did the trick for four guns. For the rest of the day we walked on air!

The woodcock is strong meat, although some connoisseurs will go a long way to taste it. It must be peculiarly strong for very few dogs like picking them up. One of my friends had a dog which wouldn't touch them. Ruthlessly he tied a shot woodcock into its mouth, and made it walk at heel all the morning. I do not know what the moral may be, but ever after it retrieved woodcock as though they were the sweetest scent it knew!

I had one curious and satisfying encounter with a wood-cock. We were shooting above a railway cutting when I shot a high woodcock which fell into the tender of the Flying Scotsman. I just had time to signal to the driver as he flashed past, and he left the bird for me with his compliments with the station master at Berwick-upon-Tweed.

Another glorious recollection is a meeting with a stoat in its white winter coat carrying a woodcock in its mouth.

I have never really been able to master my nerves at the cry of 'woodcock forward', but that is inherited, for my father was

known to have had a whole wood driven again because one woodcock had gone back.

So when the Hunter's Moon comes round each November I visit the usual haunts of the woodcock for the pleasure of hearing the 'flip' and to confirm that the flight is 'in'.

CHAPTER VII

The Snipe

Like the woodcock the snipe can provide exhilarating sport
and the scene for the shooter's operations is the bog. They too
feed where the earth-worms are numerous, and there many of
them will stay all day.

In September the birds are home-bred and in October they
will be joined by large reinforcements from the east.

Bogs – at least the heaving pulpy kind – can be dangerous.
I once made the beginner's mistake of trying to cross such an

area on tip-toe and as fast as I could. I was soon over the waist in black, oozy slime, and had to stretch out my arms with my palms flat in order to prevent being sucked under. Luckily help was at hand. The only way to proceed when one suspects the ground is bottomless, is to step slowly from rush bush to rush bush, and then slowly with the feet flat – but retreat is sometimes wise.

There is one other preliminary warning which, unless it is heeded, will surely ruin the day. Nothing alarms a snipe as much as the human voice. I have seen a bog cleared by a gun shouting at a wayward dog, or by one of the shooters calling 'snipe' as a bird rises. The result is that they get up far out of range. The only safe rule is silence.

There are other tips which will pay a high dividend to the snipe-shooter.

When walking snipe arrange where possible that the wind is blowing from behind the guns. The snipe always rises into the wind, and when it does so the white breast and neck are exposed which will give an extra split second to get off the shot before it streaks away on its erratic course.

The next best course is to approach the birds across the wind when there is a fair chance of a broadside shot. The worst of all worlds is had by walking the snipe into the wind, for they will then take off close to the ground and start the jinking at once, presenting a ghost of a target with only their camouflaged backs to be seen.

The other secret of success is always to walk slowly. The snipe is a difficult enough target without sacrificing balance in heavy, tufty ground. Snipe-shooting is a knack, and the technique of it can scarcely be put into words, and will only come with practice. In time the shooter will recognize the sign that for a yard or so the bird will fly straight, then it is a case of up with the gun and fire; to hang on and try to follow the will-o'-the-wisp with the gun will almost always result in a miss. There is no doubt that no. 8 shot is an advantage.

The snipe in flight is given away by its call. I was ten years old when I first realized the advantage of keen ears. I was walking home with a friend of my father's and apparently the day was done. Suddenly he stopped and fired his gun, and before I had gathered my wits two tiny parachutes were descending from high in the sky. Hearing is an essential part of the snipe-shooter's equipment.

The best plan when shooting a given area is to select the main bog for the first operation. The snipe will then scatter to the smaller wet patches and ditches which local knowledge will have revealed.

The best conditions for making a bag are when a quiet night is followed by a hot day. The birds will then be well fed and will sit comparatively tight. Henry and I once experienced proof of that. There had been three days and nights of complete calm, and when we set out in the morning the temperature was already in the 70s. Henry had a spy-glass through which I could never see anything, but when we missed he would mark the bird's settling place and we would trudge after it again. The result was 43 snipe out of a possible 45. Many bigger bags have been shot, but I have never again seen a day when such a high percentage of success was even remotely possible.

On a stormy day the majority of the snipe will be restless and rise at extreme range or out of shot. It is then that the drive comes into its own. It should not be too long; two or three

hundred yards at the most, for the snipe is quick to gain height and will fly out at the sides.

As with the woodcock the guns walking on the flanks will get as much shooting as those ahead. The driven snipe is by-and-large an easier target than the bird which is walked, and one or two drives fitted into the day will always pay.

Occasionally at Douglas we would see a great snipe; they are very rare and should be spared; but when the jack snipe arrives there are always enough to add one or two to the bad when variety is required.

The increased and elaborate draining of low land is fast reducing the concentrations of snipe in Scotland; for when the pulpy, slimy mud is creamed off the surface of the bog it will no longer find favour. For those who were not too fastidious the old-fashioned sewage farms used to provide fine shooting, but they too are disappearing.

But if the sportsman knows how to look for the damp place where the cows are encouraging the worms (and if he can afford the cartridges) there are still enough snipe, when the migrants arrive in October, to provide some good shooting.

Anyhow there are sufficient to supply the connoisseur's delight which is a cold snipe with a poached egg for his breakfast.

CHAPTER VIII

The Golden Plover

At Douglas, when I was a boy, there used to be a flock of golden plover on almost every farm, and it would number between twenty and a hundred. Now one is lucky to see a dozen in a shooting season. The reason is clear. The 'golden' likes fields where the grass is poor, and the ragwort and other weeds abound. There the birds used to scuttle (they do not hop or run) in pursuit of the leather-jackets, and the caterpillars of the cinnabar and the six-spotted burnet moths which tumble off the yellow ragwort plants. Now few farmers will tolerate

[69]

such a field, the fertilizers ensure that the grass is lush, and such abundance and luxury the golden plover will not patronize.

They are a loss to the shooter because, when there was no grouse-shooting due to bad weather, they provided the ideal diversion for two or three guns to try and outwit them by stalking or by improvised drives. Hours could be 'wasted' that way.

The 'golden' is wild and wary, but curiosity can be its downfall and there are some ruses which the shooter can adopt to get within range. The best is to walk in narrowing circles round the flock, bending down from time to time as though picking mushrooms. That will often work, and the chances of success are increased if the gun has a well-trained dog which will work to heel. Golden plover and ducks seem to be hypnotized by a dog which shows itself intermittently and they will run or swim towards it.

Then, where there are plover, there are usually cows. If one can be induced to chaperon the stalker it is possible to get close to the birds.

I recall doing this one day with my House-Master from Eton. He took one horn while I held the tail. A cow can be a vicious kicker, but as long as one walks directly behind it one is safe, as it always kicks sideways. On that occasion we arrived right in the middle of a large gathering of plover.

The third possibility is to whistle for the birds, imitating the two plaintive notes of the 'golden's' call. Early in the season that deception will often bring them within shot, but it invites sore lips.

The last possibility – when all else has failed, and the golden plover are flying overhead but out of range – is to fire a shot ahead of the leading birds. They will then dive and if one has reloaded quickly it is possible to get in two barrels as they come sweeping and swirling by. It is tempting for the beginner at such a moment to 'brown' into the flock, and hope for the best. Invariably when a shooter gives way to such a base act his eye deservedly finds the empty space and nothing results. It serves him right.

I remember one amusing variant of that rule. A young and uninitiated friend of ours fired at random into a lot of 'golden', and a bird fell. On being retrieved it was a starling.

Henry on these marauds was always getting into trouble. At dinner one August night the butler bore in a note on a silver salver to my grandfather. It was from a tenant-farmer, saying that he had found pellets in the udder of his cow. It says much for the value of money in those days that ten shillings settled the matter to the satisfaction of all.

Indeed it was shortly to be proved too generous. A small boy who had been hiding under the bank of the river rose as Henry fired a shot at a snipe, clutching his ear. The lobe of the ear was not even penetrated. The magic tariff produced smiles all round. But when next we went to shoot in the same place the bank was lined with youths eager to earn such danger-money.

Happily, although we now see little of them in the shooting season, the golden plover returns to the moors in the spring. Then the cock bird is magnificent in his black satin waistcoat and his coat of gold.

Like the snipe the golden plover is delicious to eat, and is best when it is cold.

CHAPTER IX

The Mallard, the Teal and the Wildfowl

Wild-fowling is the sport which probably gives the greatest pleasure to the greatest number. It needs little formality and all that is wanted is local knowledge, an instinct for position, a gun and a dog. It can be enjoyed by an individual alone with the dawn, or the dusk, or by a party who after the shoot will exchange tales far into the night.

It is physically testing too, for on the sea-shore, or in the cover of a ditch, or in a hide in the reeds on the marsh, the elements are often harsh, indeed the gale and the sleet are the wild-fowler's friends.

In all forms of shooting a dog is a delightful companion, but in the wild and watery environment of the duck-flight it is essential, and the dog must swim like an otter. When a retriever is really skilled he will pick up the swish of the duck's wings before the human ear. He will mark the direction in which the duck falls, and bring back the runner before it can flap away into loch or river.

When there is a complete understanding between the man and his dog the latter can be trusted to slink away and do its work while the flight is still in progress, as it will lie down and freeze to the ground at the sound of wings.

My preference has always been for the black labrador, but that is a matter of taste and I have seen splendid water dogs of different breeds.

Of the two flights – morning and evening – I much prefer the dawn. At sunrise all the world of nature is waking up and full of zeal for the new day, and every bird is talking to his neighbour. Curlew and golden plover, redshank and snipe will keep up a constant chorus, and only the pigeon, usually so talkative, will come flying purposeful and silent and straight, as though breakfast is its sole purpose in life.

But great satisfaction can also be had if one can find a place of concealment on a line of the evening flight when there is a gale of wind. Then the ducks will be flying strongly but low, and an exciting half-hour will result.

At Hirsel and Douglas we are lucky, as almost all the wild-fowl come in to the lakes in the course of the winter. The only difference being that the goosander prefers the east and the merganser the west.

I once picked the bodies or backbones of thirty-two small trout out of one male goosander, and that was only the morning meal! In exasperation the fishermen organized winter shoots, the sole result of which was that a certain number of the goosanders, male and female, were winged. They then stayed to nest and to feed their young all through the summer months so that for the fishermen the last situation was worse than the first. Their nests in a hole in the river bank are difficult to find as both the drake and duck approach it with an uncanny stealth.

In the school holidays we used to seek out the barley or oat-field where the corn had been laid by wind and rain. When the mallard had found it they would swarm into it like children round an ice-cream van.

On the first night chosen for the shoot the ducks will scarcely be put off, and there will be forty minutes or so of fast shooting. It is only very occasionally that they will return in any numbers to the same field.

On such evenings a reconnaissance of the cornfield is worth-while as it is not easy when in a hurry to choose the right place in the field; nor, although the farmer is happy for the ducks to be shot, will he appreciate his corn being trampled down by heavy feet.

The essence of duck-shooting is to remain unseen until the last moment, so it is often necessary to sit or kneel. If one has not got anything so sophisticated as a three-legged stool – which is the ideal foundation for duck-shooting – a wooden box is quite an adequate substitute. Something of the kind is highly desirable as there is nothing so unbalancing as trying to

rise from one knee, and nothing so certain that if one does the swerve of the ducks and the slow response of muscles will make for poor shooting.

There are occasions on a bare stubble when it pays to lie on one's back, and it is often necessary to do so particularly in moonlight.

There is one precaution which it is always worth taking if the location allows it. It is to build a hide with a front and a back, for it is extraordinary how easily a man is spotted if he is standing behind a hedge or an improvised hurdle unless a dark background is contrived. A bank behind one serves very well, but ingenuity can usually find branches to break the sharp silhouette.

There is a whole literature of wild-fowling to which it is impossible to add anything new except possibly this. When a duck of any kind rises out of a pond or stream always aim above its head. All the duck tribe – and in particular the teal – lift out of water with the speed of a well-oiled modern lift.

My father always used to insist that ducks could smell, and he would disallow smoking in the hides round the flight pond. I have never been able to verify that, but I do know that before ducks begin to fly to a flight pond they will often send out a single scout. If it is not shot and it returns to give warning many others will stay away.

One wild-fowling day in particular has stuck in my mind. We shot in the valley of the Douglas Water river and the bag was 57 mallard and teal and 51 snipe. An American was shooting, and all he could do was to mutter 'it was great' far into the night.

I once shot on Lake Winnipeg on the opening day of the

Canadian season. The ration was 10, and with the first shot from one of the two hundred guns the sky was dark with ducks and geese. I could have got my allowance in a few minutes, so I asked my guide how many varieties inhabited the lake, and he said 13. I then told him that if he would identify the species as it flew over the butt I would try and shoot one of each. After two hours I had 11 of the possibles, and thus had a most enjoyable morning. The luncheon was so festive that no one noticed the one which was outside the law.

One mallard at Hirsel made a habit of nesting year after year in the fork of a lime tree some four hundred yards from the lake. When the eggs hatched she would be quite ruthless and push the chicks out of the nest. They would come tumbling and bouncing down the thirty-foot drop like balls of fluff, and then set out in triumphant procession down the drive.

In my year at No. 10 Downing Street a mallard duck nested in some low hypericum just outside the Cabinet Room. Eventually she left by the back door, and so a little later did I.

CHAPTER X

The Wood Pigeon

Officially the wood pigeon is vermin. Soon after the war I met a lady in the train who volunteered the information that she was a Pest Officer, and that she was concentrating on exterminating the pigeon. I asked her how she was setting about the task, and she replied that she was 'netting them'. I sat back in my seat content that the bird which had given me so many sporting days was assured of its future, and I willingly paid my share of the taxes to keep the lady in work. The female pigeon lays only two eggs at a time, in a rickety-looking nest, but she

[78]

may go through the business three times in a summer, thus ensuring that the breed is always numerous. In October, too, great flocks arrive from Norway to reinforce the home supply.

The pigeon is the wiliest of birds, and if there is one which turns more quickly at the sight of a gun I do not know it. Doubtless this facility comes from being the enemy of all who grow corn or roots or greens, but the pigeon deserves a better title than vermin.

It follows that the most important consideration in pigeon-shooting is camouflage and cover, whether the shooter is flighting them into a cornfield or into a wood in which the birds are roosting. The hide should be completed before the time for the pigeons' arrival, for nothing is more frustrating than one which is continually collapsing when the birds are coming thick and fast. A branch in one hand and a gun in the other is hardly the recipe for accuracy. A length or two of string is an invaluable aid to the stability of the improvised shelter.

The first parts of the shooter which the flying pigeons see are his face and hands. It may be messy, but blacking both with burnt cork will pay a handsome dividend – but one must remember to wash it off. Returning from a shoot one winter's evening, I stopped in Royston to ask two women the way to my destination. Their immediate reaction was to scream and run. Happily there were few people on the move and further explanations were not required.

Less hazardous and even more effective is the disguise for days when snow is lying on the ground. It consists of an old sheet with holes cut for the neck and arms. I have seen pigeons fly low and straight over the strange piebald object, so little do

[79]

they connect it with a man and a gun.

Probably the biggest bags of pigeons are made by flighting into cornfields in August. Decoying is legal, and there is a very life-like artificial bird which, at the jerk of a cord, flaps its wings. But such sophistication is not really necessary, for all the shooter has to do is to go to his stand with a dozen sticks sharpened at both ends. He can then stick one end into the lower beaks of the first pigeons he shoots, and the other end into the earth or the bales of straw. His decoys are then ready and they cost nothing.

On August and September days there are two main flights into the corn. From 9 a.m. to 12 and from 3 p.m. to 7. Between times the shooter can safely take a siesta for few will fly. My brother William once took that too literally. He had 80 by noon and never woke up!

Later in the year, in the strong winds of winter, it is possible to organize very successful shoots as the birds fly to roost in woods of thick conifers. The shooting can either be done from the ground, taking advantage of a clearing in the trees, or from a hide built in the tops of the trees when the pigeons approach like driven grouse. For purely personal reasons I prefer my feet on the ground.

On a day when a full gale was blowing, my host, in the security of the house at lunch-time, asked me if I would like to occupy a hide in the tree-tops. I accepted with alacrity, expecting a conifer plantation of twenty feet or so. On arrival my keenness evaporated. The hide was perched 50 feet up a beech tree, and approached by a frail and vertical ladder. It was useful training, for some 30 years later I was faced with a similar situation in the partially rebuilt Reichstag in Berlin.

There was the perpendicular ladder rising in empty space from the middle of the floor with a 50 foot climb to the roof in order to look into East Berlin over the infamous wall. Nothing would have got me up or down except for my previous experience, and the knowledge that if as Foreign Secretary I went to the top the world's press would be bound to follow. There were some green-looking faces that day.

My host at the pigeon-shoot was a tough fellow. As a kind of feu-de-joie he would at the start of the day load his gun and fire both barrels into the air. This time he had gone through the ritual. But his valet-loader had packed the cleaning rods in the barrels of his gun, and had forgotten to take them out.

They emerged like a couple of missiles with a shower of paper confetti, and, one of the barrels bursting, blew off a part of his thumb. There was a hideous oath and he took another gun and shot for the rest of the day – clearly someone else had to face an ordeal. With his caustic comments following me and my gun and cartridges into the heights I somehow arrived.

One of the secrets of successful pigeon-shooting is to allow the birds to get a fraction closer to you than any other species – when they turn the gun has a better chance.

Many a farmer is only too happy to allow a careful shooter to protect his crops from these intrepid birds which will refuse to be put off even by the most elaborate mechanical devices.

The best weather for the pigeon-flight is provided by a strong steady wind and squally showers. Hidden on a hill called Spylaw – for it was from there that the Scots used to reconnoitre the ground before making a raid into Northumberland – it was possible to see the pigeons streaming over the fields, and on over the Tweed until they reached the wood in Scotland in which thousands would roost. I recall one particular January in which they were devastating the winter wheat, and it was imperative to shoot them down. We placed guns carefully, in each of eight woods, and the result was 1600 pigeons in the four consecutive days. Even that scarcely made a dent in the population.

For the young shooter the pigeon gives wonderful practice, but he must be warned that with pigeons it does no good to morale to count the cartridges fired.

CHAPTER XI

The Wild Goose

The wild goose is the most romantic and mysterious of all the birds which arrive in Britain as summer turns to autumn. The first skeins of them will be seen high in the sky flying in the 'V'-shaped formation which they adopt for their long journeys from the Arctic Circle to the south. As they go they give tongue like a pack of hounds in full cry. They fly with a sense of purpose to a chosen destination, and to feeding-grounds which they have inherited from their ancestors, and to which they are faithful unless industrial man intervenes. Even then they will persist, for when at Douglas coal-drilling was introduced on the edge of their roost for the night, they made a reconnaissance and settled down for the winter only just outside the circumference of the shining lights and noisy clatter.

The dawn flight for geese is the elixir of wild-fowling, and the first honk when it is as yet too dark to see, sets the blood coursing. That is always welcome and sometimes positively necessary for survival. With a friend I lay out one morning in frost and ice when a flock of pinkfoot settled some two hundred yards in front of us. There was no cover and therefore no option but to crawl as far as a ditch allowed, and then to run at the geese hoping to get within range as they rose. The crawl duly accomplished we ran; my companion slipped as he rose and was never in the race. I got right into the outskirts of the flock, but my thumb was so stiff with cold it would not push up the safety-catch, nor would my forefinger bend to pull the trigger.

The following morning we decided to try again, and this time my friend's wife carried a torch to guide us to our places. Her hands became so numb that she let the torch fall, and it rolled alight down a small slope. Simultaneously there was a honk seemingly just above us. I heard a strangled hiss 'Sit on it – damn you' and she did. We had a successful flight and there was no divorce!

There is no doubt that the pinkfoot and the greylag and – from my observation in Islay – the barnacle, are rapidly increasing in numbers. Fifty years ago a goose at Douglas was a rarity, nor did I see more than the odd bird in the valley of the Tweed. Now in both places, the pinkfoot at Douglas and the greylag at The Hirsel, assemble in their hundreds. They have presumably found their traditional feeding-grounds on

Tayside to be overcrowded, and been forced to extend their range southwards. It is not surprising for, during a picnic lunch some ten miles from Perth, I saw anything up to four thousand geese come in to feed on one large barley-stubble. Too many tax the patience of the farmer, and in a wet year he suffers not only from the loss of grass and winter wheat, but from puddling which turns his fields into a sea of mud in the spring.

Lanarkshire is a county of walls, which every now and again provide enough cover for a crawl after geese of a particularly agonizing and breathless kind. Few remember that it is as necessary to keep the stern as low as the head, and I have seen many a sentinel goose watching with interest an object which looked for all the world like Lester Piggott on a racehorse, while the owner was blissfully unaware of the alarm signal which he was hoisting.

More often than not the geese will place themselves well out of shot of a wall or hedge. If that happens there is a procedure which is well worth following. Geese will always rise into the wind, and then, when faced with a sight of someone driving them, they will slide down the wind for a distance before starting the next tack on their chosen route.

A careful study of the strength of the wind and the distance of the birds from the wall will lead to a calculation of the crossing-point where the geese should come within range of the concealed shooter. It is remarkable how often such a manoeuvre succeeds.

The unluckiest goose I ever shot was in circumstances which must be unique. I had woken with a horribly sore throat, and had taken out a bottle of gargle to help me get through the day. I was actually gargling when a shadow in the bright sun

heralded the approach of a bird from behind. The gargle went
down, the gun went up, and a goose fell. On that particular
day every stalk went right and we ended with 13 pinkfoot
geese.

Sir Julian Huxley once told me that the wild goose will
tolerate the sportsman with a shot-gun, but that the rifle is
quite another thing, and if shot at from a distance by an unseen
assailant the goose will not return to the same place. It was
certainly so in the case of a farmer I know. He used a rifle on
the geese some twenty years ago and they have yet to return to
his fields.

How far can a goose see? One morning I had lain out in the
corner of an oat-field stubble, when I saw six geese flying very
high across my front over the town of Lanark. I knew the
distance to be roughly six miles. They seemed all set on the
high road to Loch Lomond. Suddenly the leader turned at
right-angles, and from that moment they came as straight as an
arrow to my decoys which in those days were legal. It was so
exciting and exhilarating that I let them settle, and then grate-

fully sent them away.

Sir Peter Scott has captured the grace and power of the goose in flight, but he would agree that no picture can convey the carnival of acrobatics and clamour of hundreds on the wing which once seen and heard can never be forgotten.

CHAPTER XII

The Hare and the Rabbit

When cartridges were cheap, and the rabbit population so plentiful as almost to represent a plague, ferreting or driving the rabbits across narrow woodland rides was the best possible training for handling a gun. In such conditions rabbiting is snap-shooting which forces a boy to be quick in changing his feet, getting his gun to his shoulder, and compels him to shoot fast. Early and elementary mistakes, like looking over the barrels, or canting them to one side, will be easily detected and put right. After such an apprenticeship the boy can graduate to any game-birds with much greater confidence than he could do in any other way.

The commonest fault in shooting game-birds is to be behind or below or both. With the rabbit it is easy to see the tell-tale puff of sand which carries conviction far more surely than the word of any instructor.

Although the rabbit was a pestilence (the keepers at Douglas, apart from their other duties, would trap thirty thousand couple a year) no one would have wished upon it the disgusting and distorting disease of myxomatosis. Some day an immunity will arrive, and then the farmer will be in real trouble, for the rabbit-catcher is becoming an extinct breed. Rabbits are vermin for (even with acknowledgement to *Watership Down*) unless they are kept under, man would be eaten out of hearth and home.

The mountain hares too are so prolific that their numbers have to be reduced. They are easy to cull as they will always run to the top of a hill. On a February day when the hares have turned white the cavalry charge up the hill is a spectacular sight, but shooting them is a duty rather than a pleasure.

There is only one way to shoot the brown hare with any enjoyment, and that is to drive the ploughs and the grasses on a cold and frosty February day. Then they really go mad and gallop flat out, and the shooting is quick and clean.

With the last hare shot the guns can be cleaned and oiled and packed away until the grouse brings the shooter again to the heather and the hills.

CHAPTER XIII

Everything
in the Game Book

This book is no catalogue of records, for many shooting parties will have far surpassed the totals, and some will have achieved more varieties, nor did Douglas or The Hirsel lend themselves to big shoots. So the mixed bags and quality were our delight.

One such day comes back to me which is packed with nostalgia.

It was 7 November 1931, and the two guns were Captain Hawker, who was the Adjutant of the Lanarkshire Yeomanry, and myself.

The bag read:

Grouse	1	Mallard	4
Pheasant	1	Teal	1
Partridge	1	Golden plover	2
Blackcock	1	Pigeons	3
Woodcock	1	Hares	2
Snipe	3	Rabbits	2

That night I took the train to London, having won the Parliamentary seat of Lanark, and from then on the columns of the game book had to take the chance of an entry slipped in by stealth between the crises of world politics.

Three more examples will illustrate the kind of shoot from which I have derived the greatest pleasure.

December 8th 1933

Grouse	36	Duck	3 (Mallard)
Black game	31		(Wigeon)
Pheasants	96		(Pochard)
Partridge	1	Golden plover	8
Woodcock	1	Pigeons	2
Snipe	1	Hares	10
		Rabbits	16

December 5th 1935

Grouse	96	Duck	10 (Mallard)
Black game	22		(Tufted)
Pheasant	26		(Pochard)
Partridge	23		(Wigeon)
Woodcock	1	Pigeon	1
Snipe	1	Various	2

December 6th 1957

Grouse	78	Duck	10 (Mallard)
Black game	29		(Teal)
Pheasant	75		(Wigeon)
Woodcock	1	Various	8
Snipe	1		

Such red-letter days are scattered through my game book. I trust that they will not become a thing of the past, and that boys in the future will waken before the dawn and be in their places and hear the duck before they can be seen, and hunt the wild things in their elements through the daylight hours. The opportunities will not be so many as I was lucky enough to enjoy in early life, but scarcity will perhaps give them an added value.

If some of the tips in the preceding pages contribute to the variety with which they come home at the end of the long day then I shall be content.

CHAPTER XIV

The Salmon

During the 1964 General Election campaign Mr Selwyn Lloyd told me that I should not describe myself as a 'fisherman' but as an 'angler'. There were, he said, 50,000 fishermen with a vote, as against 3,000,000 anglers, and that preponderance should not be ignored. I responded that, accepting his low approach to politics, I could qualify under both titles as I had used every known lure from the maggot to the driest of flies.

[93]

At my first school a few of us would fish for carp (a highly skilled business) between the patches of water-lilies, inspired by the 20-pounder said to have been taken under the over-hanging branch of an ilex tree by our teacher of mathematics. None of my contemporaries had ever seen it, and suspiciously there was no photograph, but we persevered. I cannot honestly recall that we ever caught anything at all.

As children we used to catch perch in the lakes at Douglas and at The Hirsel.

Maggots were not popular in the house, nor for that matter were worms, even when hardened in moss as they should be before they are used for fishing. But obstacles, as is often the case, provided the answer, for a length of red wool wound over the hook was as deadly a bait as anyone could desire.

The perch combined numbers with quality, and 2-pounders were by no means uncommon. After the discovery of the wool all was peace and co-operation as the sport kept us out-of-doors most of the day.

There is one useful recipe for finding worms which, when the weather is dry and the ground is hard, saves much deep digging. 'Take a tablespoonful of mustard – mix it in a tumbler of warm water and sprinkle it on an area of lawn about a yard square.' In two or three minutes the worms will wriggle to the surface and there is the angler's supply.

From the coarse fish we graduated to the trout in the Easter holidays, and very occasionally to the salmon, for sometimes on the Tweed in April or May they will rise to the March Brown.

My eldest daughter caught her first salmon at the age of seven in this way, and played it for an hour. That evening she had a temperature of 104° and my name was mud. Mercifully it turned out to be measles.

As between the salmon and the trout I hesitate to express a preference. The salmon has it for size and strength, but the trout demands on the whole the greater skill and finesse from the fisherman; although even that judgement must be qualified, for so much of the pleasure of fishing depends on choosing the lightest rod and tackle which will bring the prize to land.

As to the means of catching salmon I have become purer with age. In very high-coloured water I can endure the artificial sprat or minnow for a short time, but slinging it out and winding it in cannot compare at all with the satisfaction of a well-cast fly; nor will the thin spinning line and its elastic pull when the salmon takes compare with the electric shock which travels up the arm from a pull on the sunk fly, nor provide the suspense of the slow rise to the fly when the line floats and the fish turns and the fisherman's heart stops until the hook is firmly into the corner of the jaw.

On the Tweed we have an agreement with the owner of the opposite bank that no one fishes bait under a certain height of water. It has been very beneficial to each of us.

On some days when the sun is bright and the water low it is tempting to toss in a prawn. Sometimes the salmon are greedy – indeed so mad for it that it clearly cannot do harm. But the trouble is that it becomes an addiction, and when it has been repeated too often I have seen the fish so scared that they dashed out of the tail of the pool. After that happens the salmon will become sullen and look at nothing.

Prawning in summer is better than early-season spinning, because it can be done with very light tackle, but all in all I believe that the sunk fly in cold water, and the floating fly fished regularly when the weather is warm, give the best results.

From one particular day with a bait I confess to have derived peculiar pleasure.

The Tweed was high and the water was dark, and I bicycled two miles with my spinning rod, trace and lead, and a triangle hook assembled ready for fishing. On the bank I turned out my pockets and found that I had left my baits behind. All I had was a bottle of iodine, with which I had treated a cut on my wrist, a knife and some string. Conditions were so discouraging that I nearly returned home, but I decided to carve from a piece of hard drift-wood a lure in the shape of a small fish, and to paint its top half with the iodine, in the image of an artificial 'Black and Gold'. I carved a groove down the length of the underside – laid the gut into it so that the hook was level with the tail, and bound it on with string. With my second cast I hooked a salmon, and after two hours had six clean fish on the bank. Ever since I have checked my gear before leaving home, for I recognized luck when I saw it.

Another day with the bait I recall with mixed feelings. I lost eleven fish in the morning, and at lunch the bag was nil. In the afternoon I landed eleven without losing one. How can one account for that?

There is one rule about bait-fishing. Go on reeling when the fish takes. I once told this to a friend, but the only trouble was that I had omitted to say that at some point he must let go!

Until the last war the pride of any fisherman was his box of salmon flies, with combinations of all the colours in the rainbow. The very names were romantic – Jock Scott, Silver

Grey, Durham Ranger, Mar Lodge, Black Doctor, Blue Charm, Garry, Green Highlander and many more.

Minutes in a day's fishing are precious, but they were cheerfully spent in technical and pleasurable discussion of size and pattern of body and hackle and wing, until the final knowing choice was made. And if the chosen selection failed to lure, the whole process would start all over again with only the one eliminated.

And then some dull, unimaginative fellow discovered that he had only to pluck a tuft of black or yellow hair from his retriever, and tie it round a tube, and put a hook through it, and there was a 'fly' which would catch just as many salmon as the most gaudy of its predecessors. The results were so clear that the maker of true salmon flies went out of business.

A stoat's tail is a killer, but it is not the same thing as those masterpieces of deception which added so much glamour to the fisherman's day.

I remember one particular morning under the old régime in early November when the river was running very high and with a strong tinge of colour. The sky was heavy with rain-clouds and it was certain that there would be a further flood before the end of the day. Only the shallow pools could be fished, and even then a large sunk fly was required. After much deliberation I chose the largest size of 'Wilkinson'. The selection never had to be changed until mid-day when the river began to rise and then for the last salmon I substituted a huge fly with a white wing. The first fish took hold when it was just light enough to see the fly land on the water, and I was kept busy until noon when the flood arrived like a red wall.

There was one 38-pounder which took the fly firmly as I let it linger for an extra minute in the wake of a favourite stone, and another of 32 pounds which came racing at the fly almost as soon as it touched the surface. The nine fish that morning averaged almost 20 pounds.

The best fighters are those in the 18–25 pounds range, as the bigger fish are apt to go deep and to bore.

During my lifetime there has been one find which has added immeasurably to the pleasure of fishing, and has on many rivers lengthened the season. It is of course Mr Wood's discovery of the method of angling with the greased or floating line.

I had a chance to come to his conclusion, but failed to grasp the significance of what I had seen.

Once when I was anchored in a boat beside a gentle flow, I dangled a fly on about a foot of gut on the surface, and watched it come floating down; before it could drag a salmon came slowly up and took the fly virtually out of my hand. I was so dumbfounded that I made no reaction until the fish had turned, but when landed it had hooked itself in the corner of the mouth. It was a copy-book illustration of the method which Mr Wood adopted with such outstanding success. The technique is not only effective in late spring and summer, for in the right conditions when the air is warmer than the water, the 25-pounder of the autumn run will come to a fly the size of one's little finger nail.

One October day a young ghillie was so scathing when I changed from the sunk fly which he favoured to the smallest of floaters that I decided he needed proof or he would be set in his ways for life. I chose a pool which was like glass, on which the sun was beating down. To avoid disturbance I dropped the fly in the likeliest spot where the water glided over a point of rock. There was a great lazy roll and an exclamation of incredulity and then a 19-pounder on the bank.

Previously to the floating line we used to get results when the wind hit calm water by exactly the opposite method. We would hold the rod high, pulling in the line and racing the fly along the top of the ripples; and in that way catches were made.

There is no end to the fisherman's ingenuity, and now in Canada and Iceland there is a vogue for a technique which, by looping the cast round the body of the fly, sets it skidding

[99]

across the stream at a furious pace. It is said that it is a deadly way to kill salmon across the Atlantic, but so far it has not been proved in Scottish waters. With both of these methods the fish is forced to the surface as it takes, and the fisherman has to steel his nerve and wait for the downward turn. When that is done a higher percentage of the salmon is landed than is the case with the sunk or 'wet' fly.

There has been another change in my lifetime which has done damage to many rivers and to some famous salmon pools.

When I was a boy the Tweed would run high and clear for some days – now because of the increased drainage in the hills it is a raging torrent within hours, and it will fall almost before the colour is out of the water, so shortening the time for fishing at the best height. There is another penalty, for such is the force of the volume of water that hundreds of tons of gravel are brought from the upper reaches and, being deposited in the calmer salmon pools, smother the rocky lies which the salmon favour. Nothing can be done about this development as the hill-farmer must have his drainage, but to the fisherman it is all a loss as my ancestor had foreseen.

There has been yet another change in the habit of the salmon, the significance of which is not so clear. Every thirty or forty years the spring run dwindles to a trickle, and the Tweed becomes an autumn river, then at the end of a similar period it reverts again. Other rivers have experienced the same sort of cycle. When the change takes place the smaller spring salmon seem to delay their run until the autumn when the big fish have traditionally arrived. The result is that there is a higher proportion of small fish than there used to be.

The records of the first half of the nineteenth century make no mention of the 'disease' which is the worst scourge from which the salmon of today suffer. But my grandfather used to talk of the 'itch' which would often attack them at the end of April and in the month of May. I remember it well for almost every salmon in the river would jump continuously, skating along the top of the water as though to scratch off some irritating tickle. They used to have minute ulcers on the head and the belly would look pink. During three weeks or so only the odd one would take, but at the end of that time all would recover and they would come freely to the fly.

The difference between then and the U.D.N. (Ulcerated Dermal Necrosis) of today is that now the disease kills a high percentage of the salmon in the river. No one knows why it is so deadly. It seems to be worse in the rivers which flow for a considerable distance through arable valleys, and it is possible that chemical fertilizers seeping into the water change in some way the balance of elements, and that this has an adverse effect on some insect and fish life.

During the first twelve years of the disease it was noticeable that in the lower reaches there was virtually no hatch of March Browns by which in early spring the river used to be covered. Weed too is much increased, and is taking a more tenacious hold.

The trout too (many of which are infected) are far fewer in number than they were twenty years ago, and this is true even of waters which are carefully protected.

So far the analysts and the researchers have come up with no answers, but whatever the cause the disease is virulent. I have seen a dead salmon with a patch on its head, while the salt-water tide-lice were still on its tail. The only hope seems to be that the fish will build some immunity, as the rabbits are doing with myxomatosis.

Why does a salmon take a fly? I hope that we shall never find the whole answer, because it could make fishing too easy, but it would be helpful to discover the answer to the question '*When* does a salmon choose to take a fly?' It is certain that it has no regular feeding-time like the trout, and it is known not to depend on food while it is in fresh water. A fish fresh from the sea is likely to take in any conditions, but for the rest I am fairly sure, from long observation, that it is almost all to do with atmospheric pressure, and that if one could feed the right data into a computer it would show that the best time to be on the water is when the barometer is rising as a depression moves away after a storm. But that is easier to say than to prove.

The other factor, although I believe the lesser, is the relationship between the temperature of the water and the air.

One of the most prolific days which I remember began with ice in the rings of the rod and a blizzard of hail and fine snow. There was nothing moving. About mid-day the temperature rose and the flakes of snow became large and soft. Immediately the salmon came on the take until the frost set in again.

Happily there are too many variables in the situation for anyone to prove very much, for if uncertainty was once removed, fishing would lose its charm.

There are really only two rules for the fisherman – or the angler. The first – keep his line in the water. One of my grandfather's guests once complained that there were no fish in a short pool, because he had seen nothing in it for a week, and had put his rod away. My grandfather had it netted on the following day and the haul was eighty-six salmon!

The second rule is to take advantage of local knowledge. I have wasted hours fishing stretches of strange rivers which looked perfect to the eye, but had never yielded more than the odd salmon. One thing the beginner should remember – it is never to look back over the shoulder to see what his line is doing behind him. If he does he will lose direction and balance and be away off-target. Throw the line back firmly and it will go out straight in front where it matters most.

CHAPTER XV

The Trout

Faced with one or the other – salmon or trout – how could one choose?

It would be difficult. The really artful salmon-fisher over the season will usually catch more than the ordinary performer, but the skilled trout-fisher will always come out well on the top. In other words trout-fishing is the more testing and delicate, so my choice would go that way. There are, too, many more trout streams than salmon rivers, so that opportunity is nearer to hand.

The wet fly is not to be despised when the water is cold and high in early spring, or when the wind is blustery and in one's face. But when using it the fisherman is fishing blind, and there will be too many pulls and jerks with nothing to show for them – not even the knowledge that it was the big one which got away.

So, early in life, before my father had equipped me with the dry fly, I decided to fish the wet fly casting it up and across the stream and holding the rod high. The effect was far more satisfactory for, with the fly being for the first part of its journey only an inch or two below the surface, it was possible to see the movement of the trout and thus more certainly to time the strike.

Ever since then I have fished with the dry fly unless weather conditions, wind and drag, have made it hopeless. When fishing for trout the selection of the fly really does matter, for it must match the natural variety to which the trout are rising.

If one is fishing a strange river knowledge of the local fancy will save a lot of frustration, for there will probably be well-established favourites for morning, evening and night and without help one might miss them all.

On the Tweed and its tributaries for example if the new-comer arms himself in the spring and early summer with March Brown (the female of the species), Greenwell's Glory, a Dark and a Light Olive, and in summer with a Black Gnat, a Blue Dun and a Red Spinner, he will be fully equipped. Well, per-haps not quite, for the local fisherman at the darkening will tie on his 'Old Hen'. She looks like a prim Victorian lady dressed in shades of grey and brown, but she is a killer, and always seems to attract the largest and the fattest trout.

The sea-trout on the Tweed are plentiful, and I have caught one as large as 16 pounds, but they are notoriously bad takers. To catch them it is not necessary to go on changing the fly, for if they refuse to look at a Butcher or a Grouse-and-Claret they will take nothing.

There are few disadvantages when trout-fishing in Scotland, for the Highland streams are incomparably beautiful, and everywhere there is fast and rippling water. But it is often tinged with peat, and it is seldom possible to see the trout which are present in the pool. It is a handicap compared to the chalk streams of England, where with Polaroid glasses it is possible to locate the fish and to see whether a trout is interested and lying near the surface, or cruising or lying doggo on the bottom. Then one can experiment, even if the lure is a nymph, for once a fish shows interest he is probably catchable and perseverance will be rewarded.

Patience is the key to successful fishing, and the trout-fisher in a hurry will ruin his chances. He should take a lesson from the heron. It will stand completely still for long periods of time waiting for the trout to come within reach, and if he has to move it will be by stealth with the minimum disturbance of the water. I have never verified the local belief that the heron's legs emit some sweet magnetic oil which attracts the fish, but certainly he is the prince of fishers.

It will always pay to take up a position from which a stretch of river can be seen before beginning to move about.

It is curious how, out of the thousands of casts which a fisherman will make, one will stand out in his memory. It happened to me on the River Test. A large brown trout was feeding regularly an inch or two below the tip of a dock leaf, which was leaning over the water from the far bank of the river. The gap between the end of the leaf and the trout's mouth was too narrow a space in which to drop the fly without drag, so that the only hope was to land it not so far up the leaf

that it would stick, but at the point where it was likely to slide gently into the water. Should that be achieved the result was sure. The distance was twenty yards plus, and the first cast seemed to be going too far when a gust of wind held the line and the fly fell as light as thistledown on the appointed spot. The rest was automatic and the scales turned at 4 pounds.

On another occasion I was fishing with three flies; one dry at the end and two wet with droppers, when two trout and a salmon hooked themselves simultaneously. The trout were led a dance!

For the Test my host does not overload me, and I go off

[107]

with a Red and Grey Wulff, a Caperer and a Red Spinner, and surreptitiously against the blank day – a nymph. And if, having made my reconnaissance I find that the trout are not moving, I take up my stance at one of the many beauty spots in that incomparable valley, and like the heron, await their pleasure.

If that sounds too aloof and high-minded I will confess that at home when I am in full control I indulge in the upstream minnow to eliminate the cannibal trout from the pools. In the months of July and August they will move into the heads of the streams by day and the shallows by night to gobble up the young of their own kind.

There is the smallest and lightest of celluloid minnows which can be cast upstream with a fly-rod, and pulled sharply downstream as soon as it touches the water. It is irresistible to the greedy trout with the long head and the hooked jaw, and used with discretion, it will ensure that the quantity of fish is regular and the quality maintained.

Loch fishing can be fun in a warm and gentle wind, and dapping in a stiff breeze will bring up the monsters from the deep. But I have a strong preference for the stream with all the tactical problems which are set by almost every pool; where one pays the price for failing to keep clear of the bushes, so intent is one on the rising trout; where the back-hand or even the underhand cast is needed to catch the regular riser under the low branch of a tree, and where, with the fish under the near bank, a late turn of the wrist will lay the fly up against the stems of the reeds.

With luck in such surroundings the kingfisher will flash by, or may be seen sitting like a jewel on a bare branch which leans over the water. He too is a fisher who stays still.

So give me a light trout rod, and the dry fly, and a stream which runs clear through moor or meadow, and I ask no more of the day.

If I had to choose between shooting and fishing I would go for the latter. It is a pursuit which is essentially quiet and all the beasts and the birds will sooner or later come and inspect the fisherman. Such pleasures can of course be enjoyed without a rod, but with it, every now and again, and sooner than later, the line tightens, and the peace is exchanged for an excitement so tense and tumultuous that every nerve tingles until the prize is won or lost. What more can a man ask of life?

POSTSCRIPT

I have been tempted to extend the scope of this book to include butterflies and moths and gardening, for they are pursuits which span the year.

Butterflies are the nearest thing to perfect beauty, and the collector will find himself active from April to October, in satisfying and peaceful places, and if he hatches his specimens from the caterpillar he has perforce to learn all about the trees and bushes and plants and flowers on which they feed.

The number of British butterflies is limited, and it is possible to catch all of the species, both home-bred and migrant, within the compass of a lifetime.

I would however be content to see and not catch the large blue as its numbers have been so sadly curtailed.

For moths it would be well to start early for there are over three thousand species which is daunting, but if I lived in the South of England I would be unable to resist the hawk moths. They are a spectacular, strong and flamboyant family in a class of their own.

Gardening had to be resisted because there is such a wealth of literature on the subject that it is not easy to think of saying anything new. But it has the great advantage that one can become a practitioner fairly late in life, and derive endless pleasure from pleasing one's fancy and propagating from one's favourites. There is something colourful for every season of the year, and even the smallest garden can give endless joy.

In the introduction to this book I forecast that the shooter and the fisherman would conclude that no day could ever be dull – include butterflies and the garden and life will be full to overflowing.